FIRST PUBLISHED 2024

FOR
WHEN
IM
GONE

A SIMPLE & THOUGHTFUL

END OF LIFE PLANNER

WITH THE IMPORTANT THINGS YOUR
FAMILY NEEDS TO KNOW

HOW TO USE THIS PLANNER

First off, thank you for picking up this planner. We know that thinking about end-of-life stuff isn't the most fun topic, but it's one of the most loving things you can do for your loved ones. This planner is designed to make that process as smooth and straightforward as possible.

SO, HOW DO YOU USE THIS PLANNER? LET'S BREAK IT DOWN:

TAKE YOUR TIME

No rush! This planner is here to help you gradually organize your thoughts and wishes. Take it one section at a time and fill out what you can. You don't have to do it all in one sitting.

BE HONEST AND OPEN

The more detailed and clear you are, the easier it will be for your loved ones to follow your wishes. Don't be afraid to be straightforward about what you want.

ADD YOUR PERSONAL TOUCH

This planner is about you, so make it yours. Add personal stories, fun facts, and little notes that reflect your personality. We've included spaces for quirky anecdotes and fun memories – use them!

REVIEW AND UPDATE

Life changes, and so might your wishes. Make it a habit to review this planner annually or whenever significant life events happen. Keeping it up-to-date will ensure your plans are always current.

SHARE WITH TRUSTED PEOPLE

Once you've filled out sections, let your trusted family members, friends, or legal advisors know where this planner is kept. The information here is vital, and it needs to be easily accessible when the time comes.

TABLE ON CONTENTS

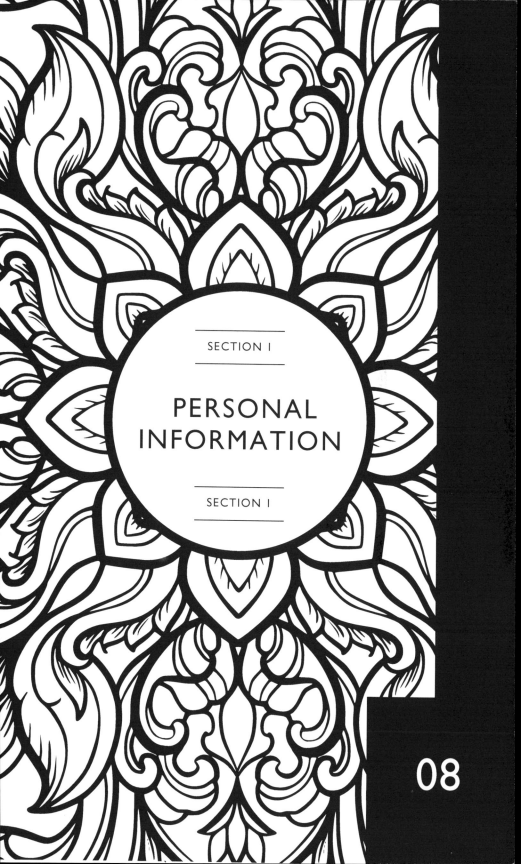

SECTION I

PERSONAL
INFORMATION

SECTION I

08

ALL ABOUT ME

BASIC INFORMATION

NAME

....

ADDRESS

....

....

HOME PHONE #   CELL PHONE #

....

DATE OF BIRTH   PLACE OF BIRTH

....

DRIVERS LICENCE #   TAX #

....

HEALTH CARD #

....

ALL EMAIL ADDRESSES: OTHER NOTES

....

....

....

....

....

PLEASE DON'T FORGET THIS...
I AM MOST WORRIED ABOUT...

IMPORTANT NOTES
ABOUT ME

IMPORTANT NOTES ABOUT ME

FUN FACTS ABOUT ME

WHAT ARE YOUR FAVORITE HOBBIES OR ACTIVITIES YOU ENJOY?

DO YOU HAVE ANY UNUSUAL OR UNIQUE HOBBIES?

WHAT IS THE MOST MEMORABLE PLACE YOU'VE EVER VISITED?

WHICH DESTINATION IS STILL ON YOUR TRAVEL BUCKET LIST?

WHAT IS YOUR FAVORITE MEAL OR CUISINE?

WHAT PERSONAL ACHIEVEMENT ARE YOU MOST PROUD OF?

FUN FACTS ABOUT ME

WHAT IS YOUR ALL-TIME FAVORITE BOOK OR AUTHOR?

WHICH MOVIE OR TV SHOW CAN YOU WATCH OVER AND OVER AGAIN?

WHAT IS ONE OF YOUR HAPPIEST MEMORIES?

IS THERE A FUNNY OR EMBARRASSING STORY YOU LOVE TO SHARE?

DO YOU HAVE A MOTTO OR MANTRA?

WHAT IS THE MOST IMPORTANT LESSON YOU'VE LEARNED IN LIFE?

ALL ABOUT MY PARTNER

BASIC INFORMATION

NAME

....

ADDRESS

....

....

HOME PHONE #   CELL PHONE #

....

DATE OF BIRTH   PLACE OF BIRTH

....

DRIVERS LICENCE #   TAX #

....

HEALTH CARD #

....

ALL EMAIL ADDRESSES:

....

....

....

....

....

OTHER NOTES

IMPORTANT NOTES
ABOUT MY PARTNER

IMPORTANT NOTES
ABOUT MY CHILDREN

ALL ABOUT MY CHILD

BASIC INFORMATION

NAME

....

ADDRESS

....

....

HOME PHONE #   CELL PHONE #

....

DATE OF BIRTH   PLACE OF BIRTH

....

DRIVERS LICENCE #   TAX #

....

HEALTH CARD #

....

ALL EMAIL ADDRESSES:

....

....

....

....

OTHER NOTES

ALL ABOUT MY CHILD

BASIC INFORMATION

NAME

....

ADDRESS

....

....

HOME PHONE #   CELL PHONE #

....

DATE OF BIRTH   PLACE OF BIRTH

....

DRIVERS LICENCE #   TAX #

....

HEALTH CARD #

....

ALL EMAIL ADDRESSES:

....

....

....

....

....

OTHER NOTES

ALL ABOUT MY CHILD

BASIC INFORMATION

NAME

....

ADDRESS

....

....

HOME PHONE #   CELL PHONE #

....

DATE OF BIRTH   PLACE OF BIRTH

....

DRIVERS LICENCE #   TAX #

....

HEALTH CARD #

....

OTHER NOTES

ALL EMAIL ADDRESSES:

....

....

....

....

ALL ABOUT MY CHILD

BASIC INFORMATION

NAME

....

ADDRESS

....

....

HOME PHONE #   CELL PHONE #

....

DATE OF BIRTH   PLACE OF BIRTH

....

DRIVERS LICENCE #   TAX #

....

HEALTH CARD #

....

ALL EMAIL ADDRESSES:

....

....

....

....

....

OTHER NOTES

ALL ABOUT MY CHILD

BASIC INFORMATION

NAME

....

ADDRESS

....

....

HOME PHONE #   CELL PHONE #

....

DATE OF BIRTH   PLACE OF BIRTH

....

DRIVERS LICENCE #   TAX #

....

HEALTH CARD #

....

ALL EMAIL ADDRESSES:

....

....

....

....

OTHER NOTES

IMPORTANT NOTES
ABOUT MY PETS

ALL ABOUT MY PET

BASIC INFORMATION

NAME

SPECIES/BREED

....

....

AGE

VACCINATION STATUS

DESEXED?

....

....

....

VET NAME + NUMBER

MICROCHIP #

....

....

MEDICAL NOTES

FEEDING NOTES

GROOMING NOTES

MY WISHES FOR MY PET

I HAVE ORGANISED THIS
PERSON TO TAKE MY PET

....

CONTACT NUMBER

....

ALL ABOUT MY PET

BASIC INFORMATION

NAME

SPECIES/BREED

....

....

AGE

VACCINATION STATUS

DESEXED?

....

....

....

VET NAME + NUMBER

MICROCHIP #

....

....

MEDICAL NOTES

FEEDING NOTES

GROOMING NOTES

MY WISHES FOR MY PET

I HAVE ORGANISED THIS
PERSON TO TAKE MY PET

....

CONTACT NUMBER

....

ALL ABOUT MY PET

BASIC INFORMATION

NAME

SPECIES/BREED

....

....

AGE

VACCINATION STATUS

DESEXED?

....

....

....

VET NAME + NUMBER

MICROCHIP #

....

....

MEDICAL NOTES

FEEDING NOTES

GROOMING NOTES

MY WISHES FOR MY PET

I HAVE ORGANISED THIS
PERSON TO TAKE MY PET

....

CONTACT NUMBER

....

ALL ABOUT MY PET

BASIC INFORMATION

NAME

SPECIES/BREED

....

AGE

VACCINATION STATUS   DESEXED?

....

VET NAME + NUMBER

MICROCHIP #

....

MEDICAL NOTES

FEEDING NOTES

GROOMING NOTES

MY WISHES FOR MY PET

I HAVE ORGANISED THIS
PERSON TO TAKE MY PET

....

CONTACT NUMBER

....

VETERINARY INFORMATION

PRIMARY VETERINARIAN

CLINIC NAME

VETERINARIAN'S NAME

ADDRESS

HOME PHONE #

CELL PHONE #

EMERGENCY VETERINARY CARE

24-HOUR EMERGENCY CLINIC

ADDRESS

HOME PHONE #

CELL PHONE #

FAMILY MEMBER
CONTACT DETAILS

NAME

....

ADDRESS

....

PHONE #   EMAIL

....

NAME

....

ADDRESS

....

PHONE #   EMAIL

....

NAME

....

ADDRESS

....

PHONE #   EMAIL

....

FAMILY MEMBER
CONTACT DETAILS

NAME

....

ADDRESS

....

PHONE #   EMAIL

....

NAME

....

ADDRESS

....

PHONE #   EMAIL

....

NAME

....

ADDRESS

....

PHONE #   EMAIL

....

FRIENDS
CONTACT DETAILS

NAME

....

ADDRESS

....

PHONE #   EMAIL

....

NAME

....

ADDRESS

....

PHONE #   EMAIL

....

NAME

....

ADDRESS

....

PHONE #   EMAIL

....

FRIENDS
CONTACT DETAILS

NAME

....

ADDRESS

....

PHONE #   EMAIL

....

NAME

....

ADDRESS

....

PHONE #   EMAIL

....

NAME

....

ADDRESS

....

PHONE #   EMAIL

....

LEGAL
CONTACT DETAILS

NAME

....

ADDRESS

....

PHONE #   EMAIL

....

NAME

....

ADDRESS

....

PHONE #   EMAIL

....

NAME

....

ADDRESS

....

PHONE #   EMAIL

....

MEDICAL
CONTACT DETAILS

NAME

....

ADDRESS

....

PHONE #   EMAIL

....

NAME

....

ADDRESS

....

PHONE #   EMAIL

....

NAME

....

ADDRESS

....

PHONE #   EMAIL

....

EMERGENCY
CONTACT DETAILS

NAME

....

ADDRESS

....

PHONE #   EMAIL

....

NAME

....

ADDRESS

....

PHONE #   EMAIL

....

NAME

....

ADDRESS

....

PHONE #   EMAIL

....

MISCELLANEOUS
CONTACT DETAILS

NAME

....

ADDRESS

....

PHONE #

....

EMAIL

....

NAME

....

ADDRESS

....

PHONE #

....

EMAIL

....

NAME

....

ADDRESS

....

PHONE #

....

EMAIL

....

IMPORTANT NOTES
ABOUT MY CONTACTS

IMPORTANT NOTES
ABOUT MY CONTACTS

SECTION 2

HEALTH
& HISTORY

SECTION 2

MEDICAL HISTORY
MAJOR ILLNESSES OR SURGERIES

DATE

ILLNESS / SURGERY DETAILS

TREATED BY

NOTES

CURRENT MEDICATIONS

MEDICATION

PRESCRIBED BY

DOSAGE & FREQUENCY

TREATMENT FOR

MEDICATION

PRESCRIBED BY

DOSAGE & FREQUENCY

TREATMENT FOR

MEDICATION

PRESCRIBED BY

DOSAGE & FREQUENCY

TREATMENT FOR

MEDICAL HISTORY
VACCINATION RECORD

DATE

VACCINATION TYPE

COMPANY

SYMPTOMS OR SIDE EFFECTS

DATE

VACCINATION TYPE

COMPANY

SYMPTOMS OR SIDE EFFECTS

DATE

VACCINATION TYPE

COMPANY

SYMPTOMS OR SIDE EFFECTS

DATE

VACCINATION TYPE

COMPANY

SYMPTOMS OR SIDE EFFECTS

MEDICAL HISTORY
FAMILY MEDICAL HISTORY

FAMILY MEMBER

NOTES

CONDITION

FAMILY MEMBER

NOTES

CONDITION

FAMILY MEMBER

NOTES

CONDITION

FAMILY MEMBER

NOTES

CONDITION

HEALTHCARE PREFERENCES

PRIMARY CARE PHYSICIAN

NAME

ADDRESS

PHONE #   EMAIL

PREFERRED HOSPITAL

NAME

ADDRESS

PHONE #   EMAIL

PREFERRED PHARMACY

NAME

ADDRESS

PHONE #   EMAIL

HEALTH INSURANCE INFORMATION

HEALTH INSURER

PHONE #   WEBSITE

INSURANCE POLICY NUMBER   GROUP NUMBER

NAME OF POLICY HOLDER

NOTES

ADVANCE DIRECTIVES
LIVING WILL

FULL NAME   DATE OF BIRTH

....

ADDRESS

....

STATEMENT OF INTENT

I, [Full Name], being of sound mind, voluntarily make this living will to express my wishes regarding medical treatment if I become incapacitated and am unable to communicate my decisions. This document reflects my preferences for medical care and is to be followed by my healthcare providers, family, and any appointed healthcare agent or proxy.

MEDICAL TREATMENT PREFERENCES
Life-Sustaining Treatment:
- I   DO   DO NOT   *(circle one)* want life-sustaining treatments such as mechanical ventilation, resuscitation (CPR), and feeding tubes if I am in a terminal condition or in a persistent vegetative state.

End-of-Life Care:
- I   WISH   DO NOT WISH   *(circle one)* to receive treatments to prolong my life if I am terminally ill. I prefer to focus on comfort and quality of life through palliative and hospice care.

Do Not Resuscitate (DNR):
- I   DO   DO NOT   *(circle one)* want resuscitation in the event of cardiac or respiratory arrest.

Organ Donation:
- I   DO   DO NOT   *(circle one)* wish to donate my organs and tissues for transplantation or medical research.

ADVANCE DIRECTIVES
LIVING WILL

SPECIFIC INSTRUCTIONS

PERMANENT UNCONSCIOUSNESS:
- If I am in a permanent vegetative state or other condition of permanent unconsciousness, I   DO   DO NOT   *(circle one)* want life-sustaining treatment.

SEVERE BRAIN DAMAGE OR TERMINAL CONDITION:
- If I have severe brain damage or a terminal illness with no hope of recovery, I DO   DO NOT   *(circle one)* want life-sustaining treatment.

PAIN MANAGEMENT
I   WISH   DO NOT WISH   *(circle one)* to receive pain relief and comfort care, even if it may hasten my death.

RELIGIOUS OR MORAL BELIEFS
My religious or moral beliefs that may influence my medical treatment preferences are:

ADVANCE DIRECTIVES
LIVING WILL

DESIGNATION OF HEALTHCARE PROXY

While this living will outlines my preferences, I have designated

[   ]

as my healthcare proxy to make decisions on my behalf if I am unable to do so.

> BY SIGNING BELOW, I ACKNOWLEDGE THAT I
> UNDERSTAND THE CONTENTS OF THIS DOCUMENT AND
> THAT I AM MAKING THESE DECISIONS VOLUNTARILY.

FULL NAME   DATE

SIGNATURE   ADDRESS

WITNESS I   DATE

SIGNATURE   ADDRESS

WITNESS 2   DATE

SIGNATURE   ADDRESS

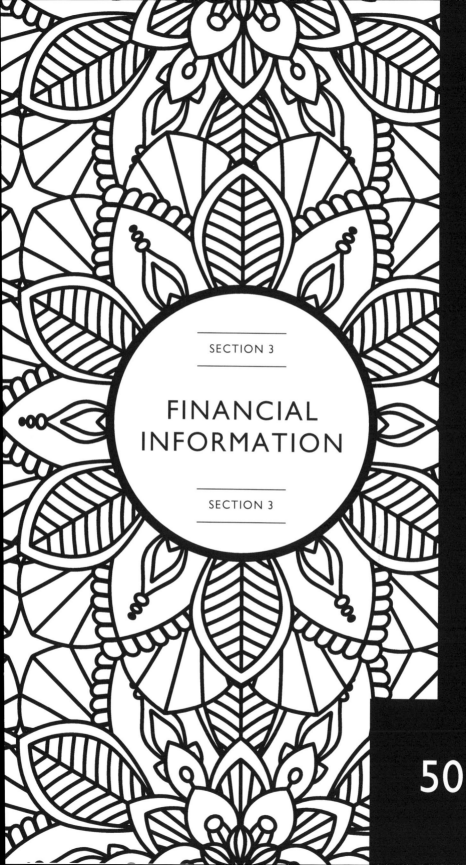

SECTION 3

FINANCIAL
INFORMATION

SECTION 3

INVESTMENTS

CHECKING ACCOUNTS

BANK NAME	
BRANCH	
BSB #	
ACCOUNT #	
SWIFT CODE IF APPLICABLE	

BANK NAME	
BRANCH	
BSB #	
ACCOUNT #	
SWIFT CODE	

BANK NAME	
BRANCH	
BSB #	
ACCOUNT #	
SWIFT CODE	

CHECKING ACCOUNTS

BANK NAME	
BRANCH	
BSB #	
ACCOUNT #	
SWIFT CODE IF APPLICABLE	

BANK NAME	
BRANCH	
BSB #	
ACCOUNT #	
SWIFT CODE	

BANK NAME	
BRANCH	
BSB #	
ACCOUNT #	
SWIFT CODE	

SAVING ACCOUNTS

BANK NAME	
BRANCH	
BSB #	
ACCOUNT #	
SWIFT CODE IF APPLICABLE	

BANK NAME	
BRANCH	
BSB #	
ACCOUNT #	
SWIFT CODE	

BANK NAME	
BRANCH	
BSB #	
ACCOUNT #	
SWIFT CODE	

SAVING ACCOUNTS

BANK NAME	
BRANCH	
BSB #	
ACCOUNT #	
SWIFT CODE IF APPLICABLE	

BANK NAME	
BRANCH	
BSB #	
ACCOUNT #	
SWIFT CODE	

BANK NAME	
BRANCH	
BSB #	
ACCOUNT #	
SWIFT CODE	

ONLINE BANKING

WEBSITE

USERNAME

PASSWORD

NOTES

WEBSITE

USERNAME

PASSWORD

NOTES

WEBSITE

USERNAME

PASSWORD

NOTES

SAFE DEPOSIT BOX

BANK

BRANCH

PROCESS

NOTES

BANK

BRANCH

PROCESS

NOTES

BANK

BRANCH

PROCESS

NOTES

STOCKS

STOCK NAME	STOCK NAME
NUMBER OF SHARES	NUMBER OF SHARES
PURCHASE DATE	PURCHASE DATE
PURCHASE PRICE / CURRENT VALUE	PURCHASE PRICE / CURRENT VALUE

STOCK NAME	STOCK NAME
NUMBER OF SHARES	NUMBER OF SHARES
PURCHASE DATE	PURCHASE DATE
PURCHASE PRICE / CURRENT VALUE	PURCHASE PRICE / CURRENT VALUE

STOCK NAME	STOCK NAME
NUMBER OF SHARES	NUMBER OF SHARES
PURCHASE DATE	PURCHASE DATE
PURCHASE PRICE / CURRENT VALUE	PURCHASE PRICE / CURRENT VALUE

BONDS

BOND NAME	
FACE VALUE	
INTEREST RATE	MATURITY DATE
PURCHASE PRICE	CURRENT VALUE

BOND NAME	
FACE VALUE	
INTEREST RATE	MATURITY DATE
PURCHASE PRICE	CURRENT VALUE

BOND NAME	
FACE VALUE	
INTEREST RATE	MATURITY DATE
PURCHASE PRICE	CURRENT VALUE

BOND NAME	
FACE VALUE	
INTEREST RATE	MATURITY DATE
PURCHASE PRICE	CURRENT VALUE

BOND NAME	
FACE VALUE	
INTEREST RATE	MATURITY DATE
PURCHASE PRICE	CURRENT VALUE

BOND NAME	
FACE VALUE	
INTEREST RATE	MATURITY DATE
PURCHASE PRICE	CURRENT VALUE

OTHER

NAME			NAME		

NAME			NAME		

NAME			NAME		

INVESTMENTS
OTHER

NAME	NAME

NAME	NAME

NAME	NAME

PRIMARY RESIDENCE

PHOTOS

ADDRESS

PURCHASE DATE

PURCHASE PRICE

ESTIMATED MARKET VALUE

WAS THIS EVER AN
INVESTMENT PROPERTY?

◯ YES   ◯ NO

MORTGAGE DETAILS

BANK NAME	
BRANCH	
BSB #	
ACCOUNT #	
AMOUNT OWING	
INTEREST RATE %	

INVESTMENT PROPERTY

ADDRESS

PURCHASE DATE

PURCHASE PRICE

ESTIMATED MARKET VALUE

WAS THIS EVER AN
INVESTMENT PROPERTY?

◯ YES   ◯ NO

MORTGAGE DETAILS

BANK NAME	
BRANCH	
BSB #	
ACCOUNT #	
AMOUNT OWING	
INTEREST RATE %	

INVESTMENT PROPERTY

PHOTOS

ADDRESS

....

PURCHASE DATE

PURCHASE PRICE

....

ESTIMATED MARKET VALUE

WAS THIS EVER AN
INVESTMENT PROPERTY?

◯ YES   ◯ NO

....

MORTGAGE DETAILS

BANK NAME	
BRANCH	
BSB #	
ACCOUNT #	
AMOUNT OWING	
INTEREST RATE %	

INVESTMENT PROPERTY

PHOTOS

ADDRESS

PURCHASE DATE

PURCHASE PRICE

ESTIMATED MARKET VALUE

WAS THIS EVER AN
INVESTMENT PROPERTY?

◯ YES   ◯ NO

MORTGAGE DETAILS

BANK NAME	
BRANCH	
BSB #	
ACCOUNT #	
AMOUNT OWING	
INTEREST RATE %	

INVESTMENT PROPERTY

PHOTOS

ADDRESS

PURCHASE DATE

PURCHASE PRICE

ESTIMATED MARKET VALUE

WAS THIS EVER AN
INVESTMENT PROPERTY?

◯ YES   ◯ NO

MORTGAGE DETAILS

BANK NAME	
BRANCH	
BSB #	
ACCOUNT #	
AMOUNT OWING	
INTEREST RATE %	

INVESTMENTS

RETIREMENT FUND

RETIREMENT ACCOUNTS

PROVIDER   CONTACT

ACCOUNT NUMBER   CURRENT BALANCE

ASSOCIATED COSTS   PAID BY CARD OR BANK

NOTES

RETIREMENT FUND

RETIREMENT ACCOUNTS

PROVIDER

CONTACT

ACCOUNT NUMBER

CURRENT BALANCE

ASSOCIATED COSTS

PAID BY CARD OR BANK

NOTES

PRIMARY RESIDENCE

PHOTOS

ADDRESS

PURCHASE DATE

PURCHASE PRICE

ESTIMATED MARKET VALUE

WAS THIS EVER AN
INVESTMENT PROPERTY?

◯ YES　　◯ NO

MORTGAGE DETAILS

BANK NAME	
BRANCH	
BSB #	
ACCOUNT #	
AMOUNT OWING	
INTEREST RATE %	

DEBTS &
LIABILITIES

PERSONAL LOANS

LENDER	
LOAN NUMBER	
ORIGINAL LOAN AMOUNT	
AMOUNT OWING	
MONTHLY PAYMENT	
INTEREST RATE %	

LENDER	
LOAN NUMBER	
ORIGINAL LOAN AMOUNT	
AMOUNT OWING	
MONTHLY PAYMENT	
INTEREST RATE %	

LENDER	
LOAN NUMBER	
ORIGINAL LOAN AMOUNT	
AMOUNT OWING	
MONTHLY PAYMENT	
INTEREST RATE %	

AUTO LOANS

LENDER	
LOAN NUMBER	
ORIGINAL LOAN AMOUNT	
AMOUNT OWING	
MONTHLY PAYMENT	
INTEREST RATE %	

LENDER	
LOAN NUMBER	
ORIGINAL LOAN AMOUNT	
AMOUNT OWING	
MONTHLY PAYMENT	
INTEREST RATE %	

LENDER	
LOAN NUMBER	
ORIGINAL LOAN AMOUNT	
AMOUNT OWING	
MONTHLY PAYMENT	
INTEREST RATE %	

OTHER LOANS

LENDER	
LOAN NUMBER	
ORIGINAL LOAN AMOUNT	
AMOUNT OWING	
MONTHLY PAYMENT	
INTEREST RATE %	

LENDER	
LOAN NUMBER	
ORIGINAL LOAN AMOUNT	
AMOUNT OWING	
MONTHLY PAYMENT	
INTEREST RATE %	

LENDER	
LOAN NUMBER	
ORIGINAL LOAN AMOUNT	
AMOUNT OWING	
MONTHLY PAYMENT	
INTEREST RATE %	

CREDIT CARDS

ISSUER	
CARD NUMBER (LAST 4 DIGITS)	
CREDIT LIMIT	
CURRENT BALANCE	
MINIMUM MONTHLY PAYMENT	
INTEREST RATE %	

ISSUER	
CARD NUMBER (LAST 4 DIGITS)	
CREDIT LIMIT	
CURRENT BALANCE	
MINIMUM MONTHLY PAYMENT	
INTEREST RATE %	

ISSUER	
CARD NUMBER (LAST 4 DIGITS)	
CREDIT LIMIT	
CURRENT BALANCE	
MINIMUM MONTHLY PAYMENT	
INTEREST RATE %	

CREDIT CARDS

ISSUER	
CARD NUMBER (LAST 4 DIGITS)	
CREDIT LIMIT	
CURRENT BALANCE	
MINIMUM MONTHLY PAYMENT	
INTEREST RATE %	

ISSUER	
CARD NUMBER (LAST 4 DIGITS)	
CREDIT LIMIT	
CURRENT BALANCE	
MINIMUM MONTHLY PAYMENT	
INTEREST RATE %	

ISSUER	
CARD NUMBER (LAST 4 DIGITS)	
CREDIT LIMIT	
CURRENT BALANCE	
MINIMUM MONTHLY PAYMENT	
INTEREST RATE %	

CREDIT CARDS

ISSUER	
CARD NUMBER (LAST 4 DIGITS)	
CREDIT LIMIT	
CURRENT BALANCE	
MINIMUM MONTHLY PAYMENT	
INTEREST RATE %	

ISSUER	
CARD NUMBER (LAST 4 DIGITS)	
CREDIT LIMIT	
CURRENT BALANCE	
MINIMUM MONTHLY PAYMENT	
INTEREST RATE %	

ISSUER	
CARD NUMBER (LAST 4 DIGITS)	
CREDIT LIMIT	
CURRENT BALANCE	
MINIMUM MONTHLY PAYMENT	
INTEREST RATE %	

RENTAL CONTRACT

PHOTOS

ADDRESS

NAMES ON LEASE

WEEKLY RENT

LEASE START DATE

LEASE END DATE

REAL ESTATE AGENT

WHERE CAN THE CONTRACT BE FOUND?

NOTES

LIFE INSURANCE

INSURER

PHONE #   WEBSITE

INSURANCE POLICY NUMBER   COVERAGE AMOUNT

COST PER MONTH   PAID BY CARD OR BANK

NOTES

HOME INSURANCE

INSURER

PHONE #   WEBSITE

INSURANCE POLICY NUMBER   COVERAGE AMOUNT

COST PER MONTH   PAID BY CARD OR BANK

NOTES

INSURANCE POLICIES
CONTENTS INSURANCE

INSURER

PHONE #   WEBSITE

INSURANCE POLICY NUMBER   COVERAGE AMOUNT

COST PER MONTH   PAID BY CARD OR BANK

NOTES

CAR INSURANCE

INSURER

PHONE #   WEBSITE

INSURANCE POLICY NUMBER   COVERAGE AMOUNT

COST PER MONTH   PAID BY CARD OR BANK

NOTES

OTHER INSURANCES

INSURER

PHONE #   WEBSITE

INSURANCE POLICY NUMBER   COVERAGE AMOUNT

COST PER MONTH   PAID BY CARD OR BANK

NOTES

SECTION 4

LEGAL
DOCUMENTS

SECTION 4

84

LEGAL DOCUMENTS

Legal documents are essential for ensuring that your wishes are carried out after your passing. This section provides detailed information about your will and testament, including its location, the executors and trustees, beneficiaries, and the distribution of your assets. By organizing this information, you can help your loved ones navigate the legal processes more smoothly.

WILL AND TESTAMENT

KNOWING THE EXACT LOCATION OF YOUR WILL IS CRUCIAL FOR ITS EXECUTION. THIS SECTION PROVIDES INFORMATION ABOUT WHERE YOUR WILL IS STORED AND HOW IT CAN BE ACCESSED.

LOCATION OF ORIGINAL WILL

PHYSICAL LOCATION

ADDRESS

SPECIFIC LOCATION (E.G., SAFE, DRAWER):

COPIES OF WILL

PHYSICAL LOCATION

ADDRESS

SPECIFIC LOCATION (E.G., SAFE, DRAWER):

COPIES OF WILL

PHYSICAL LOCATION

ADDRESS

SPECIFIC LOCATION (E.G., SAFE, DRAWER):

EXECUTORS AND TRUSTEES

EXECUTORS AND TRUSTEES ARE RESPONSIBLE FOR CARRYING OUT THE INSTRUCTIONS IN YOUR WILL AND MANAGING YOUR ESTATE. THIS SECTION DETAILS WHO THEY ARE AND HOW TO CONTACT THEM.

PRIMARY EXECUTOR

NAME & RELATIONSHIP

PHONE NUMBER

EMAIL ADDRESS

SECONDARY EXECUTOR (IF PRIMARY IS UNAVAILABLE)

NAME & RELATIONSHIP

PHONE NUMBER

EMAIL ADDRESS

SECONDARY EXECUTOR (IF PRIMARY IS UNAVAILABLE)

NAME & RELATIONSHIP

PHONE NUMBER

EMAIL ADDRESS

EXECUTORS AND TRUSTEES

ENSURE EXECUTORS AND TRUSTEES ARE AWARE OF THEIR ROLES AND RESPONSIBILITIES. PROVIDE THEM WITH ANY NECESSARY DOCUMENTATION OR INFORMATION.

PRIMARY TRUSTEE

NAME & RELATIONSHIP

PHONE NUMBER

EMAIL ADDRESS

SECONDARY TRUSTEE (IF PRIMARY IS UNAVAILABLE)

NAME & RELATIONSHIP

PHONE NUMBER

EMAIL ADDRESS

SECONDARY TRUSTEE (IF PRIMARY IS UNAVAILABLE)

NAME & RELATIONSHIP

PHONE NUMBER

EMAIL ADDRESS

BENEFICIARIES

BENEFICIARIES ARE THE INDIVIDUALS OR ORGANIZATIONS WHO WILL
RECEIVE ASSETS FROM YOUR ESTATE AS OUTLINED IN YOUR WILL. THIS
SECTION LISTS YOUR BENEFICIARIES AND THEIR CONTACT INFORMATION.

BENEFICIARY

NAME & RELATIONSHIP

PHONE NUMBER   EMAIL ADDRESS

SPECIFIC BEQUEST

BENEFICIARY

NAME & RELATIONSHIP

PHONE NUMBER   EMAIL ADDRESS

SPECIFIC BEQUEST

BENEFICIARY

NAME & RELATIONSHIP

PHONE NUMBER   EMAIL ADDRESS

SPECIFIC BEQUEST

BENEFICIARIES

BENEFICIARIES ARE THE INDIVIDUALS OR ORGANIZATIONS WHO WILL
RECEIVE ASSETS FROM YOUR ESTATE AS OUTLINED IN YOUR WILL. THIS
SECTION LISTS YOUR BENEFICIARIES AND THEIR CONTACT INFORMATION.

BENEFICIARY

NAME & RELATIONSHIP

PHONE NUMBER   EMAIL ADDRESS

SPECIFIC BEQUEST

BENEFICIARY

NAME & RELATIONSHIP

PHONE NUMBER   EMAIL ADDRESS

SPECIFIC BEQUEST

BENEFICIARY

NAME & RELATIONSHIP

PHONE NUMBER   EMAIL ADDRESS

SPECIFIC BEQUEST

BENEFICIARIES

BENEFICIARIES ARE THE INDIVIDUALS OR ORGANIZATIONS WHO WILL RECEIVE ASSETS FROM YOUR ESTATE AS OUTLINED IN YOUR WILL. THIS SECTION LISTS YOUR BENEFICIARIES AND THEIR CONTACT INFORMATION.

BENEFICIARY

NAME & RELATIONSHIP

PHONE NUMBER   EMAIL ADDRESS

SPECIFIC BEQUEST

BENEFICIARY

NAME & RELATIONSHIP

PHONE NUMBER   EMAIL ADDRESS

SPECIFIC BEQUEST

BENEFICIARY

NAME & RELATIONSHIP

PHONE NUMBER   EMAIL ADDRESS

SPECIFIC BEQUEST

BENEFICIARIES

BENEFICIARIES ARE THE INDIVIDUALS OR ORGANIZATIONS WHO WILL RECEIVE ASSETS FROM YOUR ESTATE AS OUTLINED IN YOUR WILL. THIS SECTION LISTS YOUR BENEFICIARIES AND THEIR CONTACT INFORMATION.

BENEFICIARY

NAME & RELATIONSHIP

PHONE NUMBER   EMAIL ADDRESS

SPECIFIC BEQUEST

BENEFICIARY

NAME & RELATIONSHIP

PHONE NUMBER   EMAIL ADDRESS

SPECIFIC BEQUEST

BENEFICIARY

NAME & RELATIONSHIP

PHONE NUMBER   EMAIL ADDRESS

SPECIFIC BEQUEST

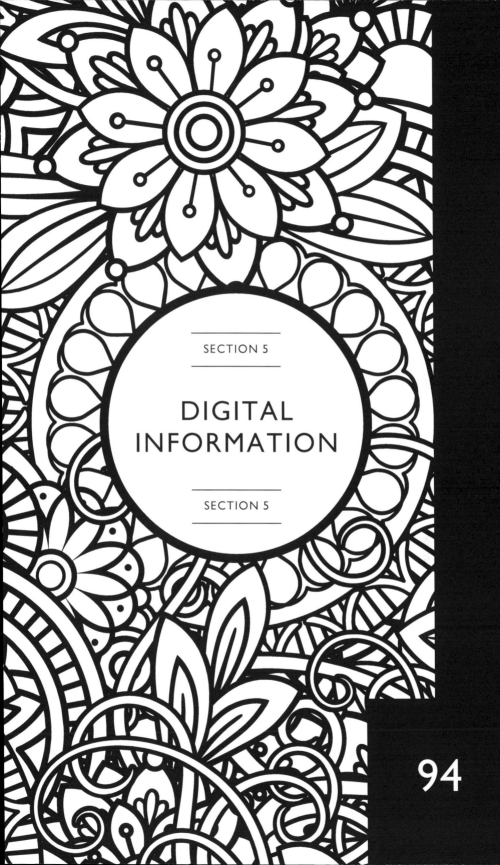

SECTION 5

DIGITAL
INFORMATION

SECTION 5

DIGITAL INFORMATION

In today's digital age, much of our personal and financial lives are managed online. Ensuring that your loved ones can access and manage your digital information after your passing is crucial. This section is dedicated to organizing your online accounts, digital assets, and providing the necessary details for smooth and secure access.

EMAIL ACCOUNTS

EMAIL ACCOUNTS ARE OFTEN THE HUB OF YOUR DIGITAL LIFE,
CONTAINING IMPORTANT COMMUNICATIONS, DOCUMENTS, AND ACCESS
TO OTHER ONLINE SERVICES. PROVIDING DETAILED INFORMATION
ABOUT YOUR EMAIL ACCOUNTS ENSURES THAT YOUR EXECUTORS CAN
HANDLE THEM APPROPRIATELY.

PRIMARY EMAIL ACCOUNT

PROVIDER

EMAIL ADDRESS   PASSWORD

SECURITY QUESTION   ANSWER

SECONDARY EMAIL ACCOUNT

PROVIDER

EMAIL ADDRESS   PASSWORD

SECURITY QUESTION   ANSWER

PLEASE ENSURE THAT ANY IMPORTANT EMAILS ARE FORWARDED TO
.... AT THIS EMAIL ....

UNSUBSCRIBE FROM ANY NEWSLETTERS OR PROMOTIONAL EMAILS.

SOCIAL MEDIA

SOCIAL MEDIA PROFILES CONTAIN A WEALTH OF PERSONAL HISTORY AND CONNECTIONS. THIS SECTION HELPS YOUR LOVED ONES MANAGE YOUR ONLINE PRESENCE BY PROVIDING ACCESS DETAILS AND INSTRUCTIONS ON HOW YOU'D LIKE YOUR ACCOUNTS TO BE HANDLED.

FACEBOOK

EMAIL ADDRESS   PASSWORD

SECURITY QUESTION   ANSWER

INSTRUCTIONS:

MEMORIALIZE THE ACCOUNT / DELETE THE ACCOUNT

INSTAGRAM

EMAIL ADDRESS   PASSWORD

SECURITY QUESTION   ANSWER

INSTRUCTIONS:

MEMORIALIZE THE ACCOUNT / DELETE THE ACCOUNT

TWITTER

EMAIL ADDRESS   PASSWORD

SECURITY QUESTION   ANSWER

INSTRUCTIONS:

MEMORIALIZE THE ACCOUNT / DELETE THE ACCOUNT

SOCIAL MEDIA

LINKEDIN

EMAIL ADDRESS   PASSWORD

SECURITY QUESTION   ANSWER

INSTRUCTIONS:

MEMORIALIZE THE ACCOUNT / DELETE THE ACCOUNT

OTHER

EMAIL ADDRESS   PASSWORD

SECURITY QUESTION   ANSWER

INSTRUCTIONS:

MEMORIALIZE THE ACCOUNT / DELETE THE ACCOUNT

PLEASE DOWNLOAD AND SAVE ANY PHOTOS AND
POSTS FROM MY SOCIAL MEDIA ACCOUNTS.

NOTIFY MY CONNECTIONS ABOUT MY PASSING
WITH A FINAL POST OR MESSAGE

SUBSCRIPTION SERVICES

SUBSCRIPTION SERVICES FOR ENTERTAINMENT, SOFTWARE, AND
OTHER ONLINE PLATFORMS CAN ACCUMULATE OVER TIME. THIS
SECTION PROVIDES DETAILS ON YOUR SUBSCRIPTIONS AND HOW
THEY SHOULD BE MANAGED.

SUBSCRIPTION

USERNAME   PASSWORD

SECURITY QUESTION   ANSWER

SUBSCRIPTION

USERNAME   PASSWORD

SECURITY QUESTION   ANSWER

SUBSCRIPTION

USERNAME   PASSWORD

SECURITY QUESTION   ANSWER

SUBSCRIPTION

USERNAME   PASSWORD

SECURITY QUESTION   ANSWER

DIGITAL ASSETS

In the modern age, digital assets form an essential part of our lives. From important documents stored online to cryptocurrency holdings and digital subscriptions, managing these assets is crucial. This section provides detailed information and instructions to help your loved ones handle your digital estate efficiently and securely.

DIGITAL ASSETS

DIGITAL ASSETS ENCOMPASS A VARIETY OF ONLINE ITEMS, SUCH AS DIGITAL CURRENCIES, INTELLECTUAL PROPERTY, AND IMPORTANT DOCUMENTS STORED ONLINE. THIS SECTION PROVIDES INFORMATION ON ACCESSING AND MANAGING THESE ASSETS.

CRYPTOCURRENCY

WALLET ADDRESS   PASSWORD

PRIVATE KEY

CRYPTOCURRENCY

WALLET ADDRESS   PASSWORD

PRIVATE KEY

DOMAIN NAME

USERNAME   PASSWORD

REGISTERED WITH

DOMAIN NAME

USERNAME   PASSWORD

REGISTERED WITH

ONLINE ACCOUNT

USERNAME   PASSWORD

WEBSITE

ONLINE ACCOUNT

USERNAME   PASSWORD

WEBSITE

ONLINE ACCOUNT

USERNAME   PASSWORD

WEBSITE

ONLINE ACCOUNT

USERNAME   PASSWORD

WEBSITE

NOTES

ONLINE ACCOUNT

USERNAME   PASSWORD

WEBSITE

ONLINE ACCOUNT

USERNAME   PASSWORD

WEBSITE

ONLINE ACCOUNT

USERNAME   PASSWORD

WEBSITE

ONLINE ACCOUNT

USERNAME   PASSWORD

WEBSITE

NOTES

ONLINE ACCOUNT

USERNAME   PASSWORD

WEBSITE

ONLINE ACCOUNT

USERNAME   PASSWORD

WEBSITE

ONLINE ACCOUNT

USERNAME   PASSWORD

WEBSITE

ONLINE ACCOUNT

USERNAME   PASSWORD

WEBSITE

NOTES

ONLINE ACCOUNT

USERNAME   PASSWORD

WEBSITE

ONLINE ACCOUNT

USERNAME   PASSWORD

WEBSITE

ONLINE ACCOUNT

USERNAME   PASSWORD

WEBSITE

ONLINE ACCOUNT

USERNAME   PASSWORD

WEBSITE

NOTES

ONLINE ACCOUNT

USERNAME   PASSWORD

WEBSITE

ONLINE ACCOUNT

USERNAME   PASSWORD

WEBSITE

ONLINE ACCOUNT

USERNAME   PASSWORD

WEBSITE

ONLINE ACCOUNT

USERNAME   PASSWORD

WEBSITE

NOTES

PASSWORDS
AND ACCESS

Passwords and access information are critical for managing your digital presence and assets. This section provides detailed instructions on how to manage passwords, access digital devices, backup information, and handle your digital legacy. Additionally, it includes some quirky tips to make this task a bit more fun.

ONLINE ACCOUNT

USERNAME   PASSWORD

WEBSITE

ONLINE ACCOUNT

USERNAME   PASSWORD

WEBSITE

ONLINE ACCOUNT

USERNAME   PASSWORD

WEBSITE

ONLINE ACCOUNT

USERNAME   PASSWORD

WEBSITE

NOTES

ONLINE ACCOUNT

USERNAME   PASSWORD

WEBSITE

ONLINE ACCOUNT

USERNAME   PASSWORD

WEBSITE

ONLINE ACCOUNT

USERNAME   PASSWORD

WEBSITE

ONLINE ACCOUNT

USERNAME   PASSWORD

WEBSITE

NOTES

ONLINE ACCOUNT

USERNAME   PASSWORD

WEBSITE

ONLINE ACCOUNT

USERNAME   PASSWORD

WEBSITE

ONLINE ACCOUNT

USERNAME   PASSWORD

WEBSITE

ONLINE ACCOUNT

USERNAME   PASSWORD

WEBSITE

NOTES

ONLINE ACCOUNT

USERNAME   PASSWORD

WEBSITE

ONLINE ACCOUNT

USERNAME   PASSWORD

WEBSITE

ONLINE ACCOUNT

USERNAME   PASSWORD

WEBSITE

ONLINE ACCOUNT

USERNAME   PASSWORD

WEBSITE

NOTES

DEVICES

PROVIDING CLEAR INSTRUCTIONS FOR ACCESSING YOUR DIGITAL DEVICES ENSURES THAT YOUR LOVED ONES CAN MANAGE YOUR DIGITAL ASSETS EFFECTIVELY. THIS SECTION INCLUDES DETAILS FOR UNLOCKING AND USING YOUR DEVICES.

PRIMARY SMARTPHONE

DEVICE MAKE/MODEL

PASSWORD/PIN   PHONE NUMBER

BACKUP UNLOCK METHOD (E.G., FINGERPRINT, FACE RECOGNITION):

SECONDARY SMARTPHONE

DEVICE MAKE/MODEL

PASSWORD/PIN   PHONE NUMBER

BACKUP UNLOCK METHOD (E.G., FINGERPRINT, FACE RECOGNITION):

LAPTOP/COMPUTER

DEVICE MAKE/MODEL

PASSWORD/PIN   PHONE NUMBER

BACKUP UNLOCK METHOD (E.G., FINGERPRINT, FACE RECOGNITION):

DEVICES

DEVICE MAKE/MODEL

PASSWORD/PIN   PHONE NUMBER

BACKUP UNLOCK METHOD (E.G., FINGERPRINT, FACE RECOGNITION):

DEVICE MAKE/MODEL

PASSWORD/PIN   PHONE NUMBER

BACKUP UNLOCK METHOD (E.G., FINGERPRINT, FACE RECOGNITION):

DEVICE MAKE/MODEL

PASSWORD/PIN   PHONE NUMBER

BACKUP UNLOCK METHOD (E.G., FINGERPRINT, FACE RECOGNITION):

DEVICE MAKE/MODEL

PASSWORD/PIN   PHONE NUMBER

BACKUP UNLOCK METHOD (E.G., FINGERPRINT, FACE RECOGNITION):

BACKUP INFORMATION

BACKING UP YOUR DIGITAL DATA ENSURES THAT IMPORTANT INFORMATION IS PRESERVED AND CAN BE ACCESSED WHEN NEEDED. THIS SECTION PROVIDES DETAILS ON YOUR BACKUP METHODS AND LOCATIONS.

PRIMARY BACKUP METHOD:

BACKUP LOCATION

HOW TO ACCESS

OTHER BACKUP METHOD:

BACKUP LOCATION

HOW TO ACCESS

ENSURE THAT BACKUPS ARE STORED SECURELY AND ARE REGULARLY UPDATED. INFORM YOUR EXECUTOR OR TRUSTED PERSON ABOUT THE BACKUP LOCATIONS AND ACCESS DETAILS

PERSONAL
WISHES
& MESSAGES

LETTERS TO LOVED ONES

Welcome to the "Letters to Loved Ones" section of your
end-of-life planner. This is a space where you can
express your heartfelt thoughts, cherished memories,
and final wishes to those you hold dear. Writing letters
to your loved ones can be a deeply meaningful and
comforting process, allowing you to leave behind a legacy
of love and personal connection.

These letters serve as a lasting testament to your
relationships, offering words of comfort, encouragement,
and wisdom. Whether you choose to write to your
spouse, children, parents, siblings, or friends, these
messages will become treasured keepsakes for your
loved ones to remember you by.

TIPS FOR YOUR LETTERS

CHOOSE YOUR RECIPIENTS

Begin by deciding who you want to write letters to. Common recipients include your spouse or partner, children, parents, siblings, best friends, and other significant people in your life.

REFLECT ON YOUR RELATIONSHIP

Take some time to think about your unique relationship with each recipient. Consider the moments you've shared, the lessons you've learned together, and the qualities you admire in them.

EXPRESS YOUR FEELINGS

Write from the heart. Share your feelings openly and honestly. Let your loved ones know how much they mean to you, express your gratitude, and share any personal messages or wishes.

INCLUDE SPECIFIC MEMORIES

Recall specific memories that highlight your relationship. These could be funny anecdotes, meaningful experiences, or moments of growth and connection. Personal stories make your

OFFER WORDS OF WISDOM

Impart any advice or wisdom you've gained over the years. This could be life lessons, encouragement for the future, or simply words of love and support.

DEAR

_____

_____

_____

_____

_____

_____

_____

_____

_____

_____

_____

_____

_____

_____

_____

FROM

_____

DEAR

FROM

DEAR

FROM

DEAR

FROM

DEAR

_____

_____

_____

_____

_____

_____

_____

_____

_____

_____

_____

_____

_____

_____

_____

FROM

_____

DEAR

_____

_____

_____

_____

_____

_____

_____

_____

_____

_____

_____

_____

_____

_____

_____

FROM

_____

DEAR

FROM

DEAR

FROM

MEMORIAL
PREFERENCES

This section is dedicated to outlining your preferences for your memorial service. Here, you can specify the type of service you would like, whether it be a traditional funeral, a memorial service, a celebration of life, or another form of gathering. Your wishes will help guide your loved ones in creating a meaningful and respectful event that honors your life and legacy.

MY MEMORIAL
DETAILS

TYPE OF SERVICE

○ TRADITIONAL FUNERAL

○ MEMORIAL SERVICE

○ CELEBRATION OF LIFE

○ OTHER: ....

LOCATION

NAME OF VENUE

....

CONTACT PERSON

....

SPECIAL INSTRUCTIONS

....

....

ADDRESS

....

....

....

SERVICE OFFICIANT

NAME

....

CONTACT INFORMATION

....

RELATIONSHIP TO YOU

....

OTHER NOTES

MY MEMORIAL
MUSIC AND READINGS

MUSIC AND READINGS CAN BE POWERFUL ELEMENTS OF A MEMORIAL SERVICE, EVOKING MEMORIES AND EMOTIONS THAT CELEBRATE YOUR LIFE. IN THIS SECTION, YOU CAN SPECIFY THE SONGS AND READINGS THAT ARE MEANINGFUL TO YOU AND THAT YOU WOULD LIKE INCLUDED IN YOUR SERVICE. THIS CAN PROVIDE COMFORT AND INSPIRATION TO YOUR LOVED ONES AS THEY HONOR YOUR MEMORY.

SONG TITLE   ARTIST

SONG TITLE   ARTIST

SONG TITLE   ARTIST

SONG TITLE   ARTIST

SONG TITLE   ARTIST

SONG TITLE   ARTIST

OTHER NOTES

MY MEMORIAL
MUSIC AND READINGS

READING

READER

READING

READER

READING

READER

READING

READER

READING

READER

READING

READER

OTHER NOTES

MY MEMORIAL
MUSIC AND READINGS

READING   READER

....

READING   READER

....

READING   READER

....

READING   READER

....

READING   READER

....

READING   READER

....

OTHER NOTES

MY MEMORIAL
MEMORIAL DECORATION

THE DECORATIONS AT YOUR MEMORIAL SERVICE CAN HELP CREATE A WARM AND INVITING ATMOSPHERE THAT REFLECTS YOUR PERSONALITY AND STYLE. IN THIS SECTION, YOU CAN SPECIFY YOUR PREFERENCES FOR FLOWERS, COLORS, AND OTHER DECORATIVE ELEMENTS TO ENSURE YOUR MEMORIAL SERVICE FEELS PERSONAL AND UNIQUE.

FLOWERS

COLORS & THEMES

PHOTOS & OBJECTS

OTHER NOTES

MY MEMORIAL
MEMORIAL DECORATION

THE DECORATIONS AT YOUR MEMORIAL SERVICE CAN HELP CREATE A
WARM AND INVITING ATMOSPHERE THAT REFLECTS YOUR PERSONALITY
AND STYLE. IN THIS SECTION, YOU CAN SPECIFY YOUR PREFERENCES
FOR FLOWERS, COLORS, AND OTHER DECORATIVE ELEMENTS TO
ENSURE YOUR MEMORIAL SERVICE FEELS PERSONAL AND UNIQUE.

FLOWERS

COLORS & THEMES

PHOTOS & OBJECTS

OTHER NOTES

MY MEMORIAL
UNIQUE CELEBRATION IDEAS

YOUR MEMORIAL SERVICE CAN BE A REFLECTION OF YOUR UNIQUE PERSONALITY AND THE LIFE YOU LIVED. IN THIS SECTION, YOU CAN OUTLINE ANY UNIQUE OR UNCONVENTIONAL IDEAS YOU HAVE FOR CELEBRATING YOUR LIFE. THESE SUGGESTIONS CAN ADD A PERSONAL TOUCH AND CREATE A MEMORABLE EXPERIENCE FOR YOUR LOVED ONES.

THEMED CELEBRATION

ACTIVITY OR EVENT

MEMORY SHARING

EXAMPLES

HOST A "FAVORITE THINGS" PARTY WHERE GUESTS BRING
AN ITEM THAT REMINDS THEM OF ME.
HAVE A "STORY TIME" WHERE FRIENDS AND FAMILY
SHARE THEIR FAVORITE MEMORIES OF ME.
CREATE A "MEMORY WALL" WHERE GUESTS CAN POST
NOTES AND PHOTOS.

LEGACY PROJECTS

Legacy projects are a meaningful way to leave a lasting impact and ensure that your values, memories, and wishes continue to inspire and support your loved ones. This section helps you outline your desires for charitable donations, legacy statements, and other creative ways to be remembered.

CHARITABLE DONATIONS
MY LEGACY

CHARITABLE DONATIONS CAN MAKE A SIGNIFICANT DIFFERENCE IN THE LIVES OF OTHERS AND REFLECT YOUR COMMITMENT TO CAUSES THAT ARE IMPORTANT TO YOU. IN THIS SECTION, YOU CAN SPECIFY ANY CHARITABLE ORGANIZATIONS YOU WISH TO SUPPORT AND THE DETAILS OF YOUR CONTRIBUTIONS.

CHARITY NAME

ADDRESS

PHONE NUMBER

TYPE OF DONATION

AMOUNT

IN HONOR/MEMORY OF

I WOULD LIKE MY DONATIONS TO SUPPORT

PLEASE INFORM [NAME] ABOUT THE DONATIONS MADE IN MY HONOR

NOTES

CHARITABLE DONATIONS
MY LEGACY

CHARITABLE DONATIONS CAN MAKE A SIGNIFICANT DIFFERENCE IN THE LIVES OF OTHERS AND REFLECT YOUR COMMITMENT TO CAUSES THAT ARE IMPORTANT TO YOU. IN THIS SECTION, YOU CAN SPECIFY ANY CHARITABLE ORGANIZATIONS YOU WISH TO SUPPORT AND THE DETAILS OF YOUR CONTRIBUTIONS.

CHARITY NAME

ADDRESS

PHONE NUMBER

TYPE OF DONATION

AMOUNT

IN HONOR/MEMORY OF

I WOULD LIKE MY DONATIONS TO SUPPORT

PLEASE INFORM [NAME] ABOUT THE DONATIONS MADE IN MY HONOR

NOTES

CHARITABLE DONATIONS
MY LEGACY

CHARITY NAME

ADDRESS

....

....

PHONE NUMBER

....

....

TYPE OF DONATION

AMOUNT

....

....

IN HONOR/MEMORY OF

....

....

I WOULD LIKE MY DONATIONS TO SUPPORT

....

PLEASE INFORM [NAME] ABOUT THE DONATIONS MADE IN MY HONOR

....

NOTES

CHARITABLE DONATIONS
MY LEGACY

CHARITY NAME

ADDRESS

PHONE NUMBER

TYPE OF DONATION

AMOUNT

IN HONOR/MEMORY OF

I WOULD LIKE MY DONATIONS TO SUPPORT

PLEASE INFORM [NAME] ABOUT THE DONATIONS MADE IN MY HONOR

NOTES

CREATE A MEMORY JAR

A MEMORY JAR IS A SIMPLE YET POWERFUL WAY TO KEEP YOUR
CHERISHED MEMORIES ALIVE. BY INVITING LOVED ONES TO
CONTRIBUTE THEIR FAVORITE MEMORIES OF YOU, YOU CAN
CREATE A COLLECTIVE KEEPSAKE THAT CELEBRATES YOUR LIFE
AND THE JOY YOU BROUGHT TO OTHERS.

Choose a jar or container that represents your
personality.

Provide slips of paper and pens for guests to write down
their memories.

Encourage loved ones to share specific, meaningful, or
funny memories.

Seal the jar and keep it in a special place where it can be
opened and read by family members during special
occasions or when they need comfort.

Examples of Memory Prompts:

My favorite memory of you is: _____
One thing I learned from you is: _____
A funny moment we shared was: _____

PLEASE START THE MEMORY JAR AT MY MEMORIAL
SERVICE AND CONTINUE TO ADD TO IT OVER TIME.
ENCOURAGE EVERYONE, YOUNG AND OLD, TO
PARTICIPATE

TIME CAPSULE

A TIME CAPSULE IS A UNIQUE WAY TO PRESERVE YOUR LEGACY
AND CREATE A TANGIBLE CONNECTION TO THE FUTURE. BY
SELECTING MEANINGFUL ITEMS AND MESSAGES TO INCLUDE, YOU
CAN PROVIDE A GLIMPSE INTO YOUR LIFE AND VALUES FOR
FUTURE GENERATIONS TO DISCOVER.

Choose a durable container that can
withstand the elements.

Select a safe location to bury or store the
time capsule.

Decide on a future date for it to be opened
(e.g., 10, 20, or 50 years from now).

ITEMS TO INCLUDE

Personal Letters:
Write letters to your future family members.
Include reflections on your life and hopes for the future.

Photographs:
Include photos that capture important moments in your life.
Add captions to explain the significance of each photo.

Memorabilia:
Include items that represent your interests and achievements
(e.g., medals, awards, souvenirs).

Current Events:
Include a newspaper or magazine to provide context about
the world at the time.

I WOULD LIKE THE TIME CAPSULE TO BE OPENED ON

PLEASE ENSURE THE TIME CAPSULE IS STORED
IN A SAFE, DRY PLACE.

FAMILY RECIPES

Food has a magical way of bringing people together, and family recipes are like little pieces of history passed down through generations. This section is dedicated to those cherished dishes that have graced your family table over the years. Whether it's your grandmother's secret pie recipe or your dad's famous barbecue sauce, these recipes are more than just instructions – they're a taste of home, love, and tradition.

RECIPE

INGREDIENTS

PREP TIME

SERVES

DIRECTIONS

RECIPE

INGREDIENTS

PREP TIME

SERVES

DIRECTIONS

RECIPE

INGREDIENTS

....

....

....

....

....

....

....

PREP TIME

....

SERVES

....

DIRECTIONS

RECIPE

INGREDIENTS

PREP TIME

SERVES

DIRECTIONS

RECIPE

INGREDIENTS

PREP TIME

SERVES

DIRECTIONS

RECIPE

INGREDIENTS

PREP TIME

SERVES

DIRECTIONS

SECTION 7

FINAL
CHECKLIST

SECTION 7

IMMEDIATE STEPS AFTER I'M GONE

The immediate period following a loved one's death can be overwhelming and emotionally challenging. This guide outlines the essential steps that need to be taken right after death to ensure that everything is handled smoothly and with care.

NOTIFY FAMILY AND CLOSE FRIENDS

○ Contact immediate family members and close friends to inform them of the passing.

○ Use a phone tree or group message to quickly and efficiently spread the news.

○ Provide support and comfort to those who may be deeply affected.

CONTACT HEALTHCARE PROVIDERS

○ Notify the deceased's primary care physician or attending doctor to officially pronounce the death.

○ Obtain a death certificate from the doctor or coroner.

ARRANGE FOR THE CARE OF DEPENDENTS AND PETS

○ Ensure that any children, elderly dependents, or pets are cared for and safe.

○ Contact friends or family members who can provide temporary care.

SECURE THE DECEASED'S HOME

○ Ensure the deceased's residence is secure. Lock all doors and windows.

○ Inform neighbors or the building manager of the situation.

NOTIFY THE EXECUTOR OF THE WILL

○ Contact the executor named in the deceased's will.

○ Provide them with necessary information and documents.

CHOOSE A FUNERAL HOME

○ Contact a funeral home to transport the body and begin making arrangements.

○ Provide the funeral home with necessary information about the deceased.

INFORM EMPLOYERS AND RELEVANT ORGANIZATIONS

○ Notify the deceased's employer, if applicable. Contact any relevant organizations or clubs to inform them of the death.

ADDITIONAL NOTES

KEEP A LIST OF PEOPLE WHO NEED TO BE CONTACTED AND CHECK OFF EACH AS YOU GO.

TAKE TIME TO BREATHE AND PROCESS; IT'S OKAY TO ASK FOR HELP FROM OTHERS

Made in United States
Troutdale, OR
08/27/2024